America's Deserts

Guide to Plants and Animals

Marianne D. Wallace

fulcrum kids

Golden, Colorado

To Gary, Zeb and Ben
and all the other desert explorers.

Plants and animals shown on the front cover: Joshua tree, painted lady butterfly, Indian paintbrush, desert tortoise, brittlebush, burrowing owl, California poppy, collared lizard, saguaro, black-tailed jackrabbit, Gila woodpecker, bat, lesser nighthawk.

Plants and animals shown on the back cover: Lechuguilla, coachwhip, sand verbena, woodrat, desert hairy scorpion, antelope squirrel, ocotillo, Costa's hummingbird.

Library of Congress Cataloging-in-Publication Data

Wallace, Marianne D.
    America's deserts : guide to plants and animals / Marianne D. Wallace.
       p.   cm.
    Includes bibliographical references and index.
    Summary: A color field guide to America's deserts, with watercolor illustrations and descriptions of the plants and animals that inhabit the different desert regions.
    ISBN 1-55591-268-0 (pbk.)
    1. Desert fauna—United States—Juvenile literature. 2. Desert plants—United States—Juvenile literature. 3. Desert fauna—Mexico—Juvenile literature. 4. Desert plants—Mexico—Juvenile literature. [1. Desert plants. 2. Desert animals.] I. Title.
QH104.W35   1996
574.973'0915'4—dc20   95-37050
                                      CIP
                                          AC

Printed in Korea

0 9 8 7 6 5 4 3 2 1

Fulcrum Publishing
350 Indiana Street, Suite 350
Golden, CO 80401-5093
(800) 992-2908

TABLE OF CONTENTS

Introduction to Desert Life

Imagine a place with only a few drops of water to drink all year long. A place where the sun can be so hot that rocks are too hot to touch. If this were your home, how would you survive? Where would you find water? How could you keep cool during the hot summer? The plants and animals that live in the desert have special ways of dealing with these things. They have adaptations that allow them to survive.

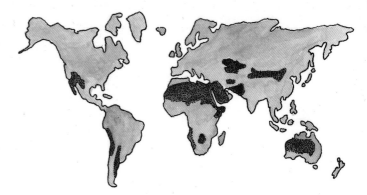

Deserts occur all over the world, covering about $\frac{1}{7}$ (14%) of the land's surface.

All deserts have very little water available for the plants and animals. The rainfall amount in a desert area averages 10 inches (25.4 cm) or less each year, and the wind and sun evaporate much of the water that reaches the ground. But plants and animals are very good at using whatever water is available. The **kangaroo rat** and **pocket mouse** get all the moisture they need from the seeds they eat and never have to take a drink of water. And desert wildflower seeds "wait" until a good rainy season … then they sprout, make flowers, set seeds and die, leaving the seeds to last through the rest of the hot, dry year until the rains come again.

Pocket Mouse

Owl's-clover   California Poppy   Phacelia   Desert-sunflower   Monkeyflower   Lupine

Deserts can also be very hot. Summer temperatures of 120°F (49°C) are common in some areas. Most animals could not survive being exposed to this kind of heat for very long unless they can find ways to avoid it. Several animals like rabbits, ground squirrels and some insects spend the hottest part of the day underground in tunnels and burrows where it is several degrees

4

cooler. Others, like lizards and snakes, might seek the shade between or underneath rocks.

Nocturnal animals such as owls, scorpions, pack rats, **kit foxes** and bats avoid the sun altogether and leave their homes to hunt for food after the sun has set. Temperatures at night can be as much as 50°F (10°C) cooler than those during the day.

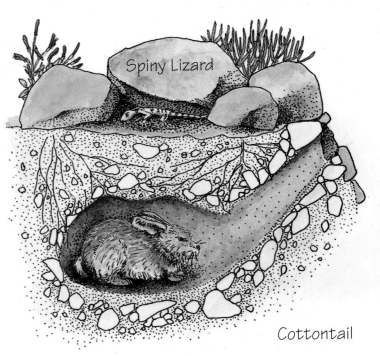

Spiny Lizard

Cottontail

The green leaves of a plant are very important because they make the plant's food. But some of the plant's water can escape through the leaves, and desert plants need to hold on to all the water they have. So the leaves of bushes, shrubs and trees that live and grow through the hot summer are often special. They may be covered in short hairs, like the **brittlebush**, to trap moisture before it can escape. The leaves of the **creosote bush** are tough and leathery with oils on the outside to keep most of the water inside the leaf. **Desert holly** is pale green during the year to reflect back some of the sunshine; in the

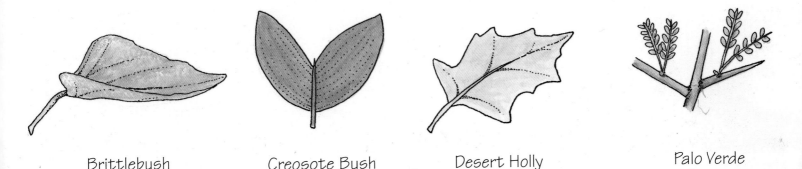

Brittlebush   Creosote Bush   Desert Holly   Palo Verde

hot summers, the leaves turn almost white to reflect even more of the sun's rays. The **palo verde** tree has small leaves that are dropped when water is not available. The tree then makes its food with its green branches (palo verde means "green stick") instead of its leaves.

Short-lived wildflowers, underground burrows, nocturnal activity, different kinds of plant leaves … these are just a few of the ways desert life survives.

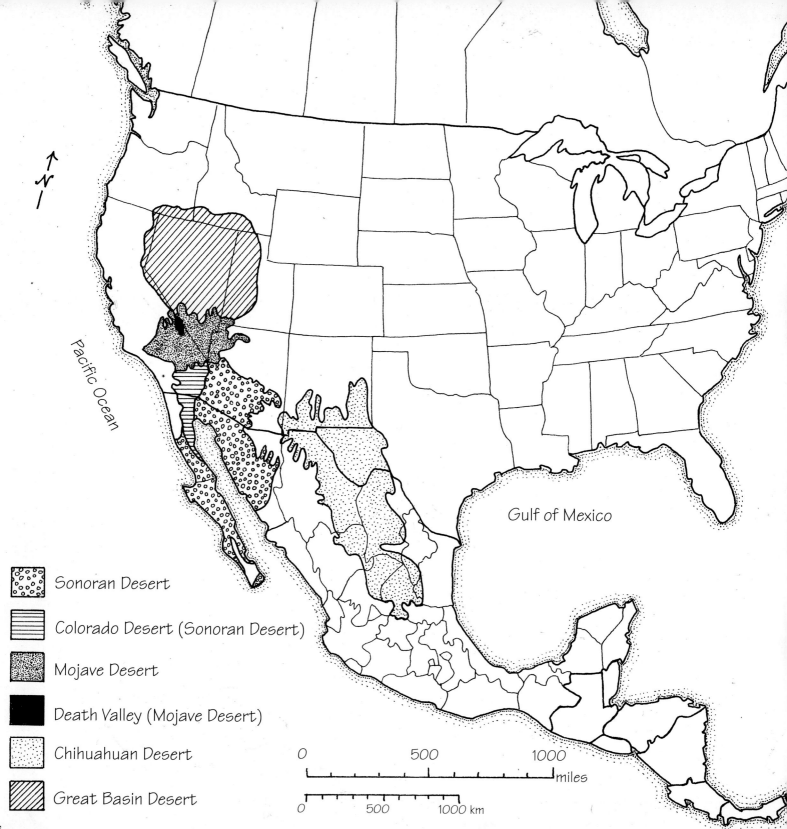

Pacific Ocean

Gulf of Mexico

Sonoran Desert

Colorado Desert (Sonoran Desert)

Mojave Desert

Death Valley (Mojave Desert)

Chihuahuan Desert

Great Basin Desert

0   500   1000
miles

0   500   1000 km

North American Deserts

There are four desert regions in North America. They are the Sonoran, the Mojave, the Chihuahuan and the Great Basin. Located in the Western United States and northern Mexico, they cover about $\frac{1}{20}$ (5%) of the North American continent. When you look at the map on the opposite page, notice that most of the deserts touch each other. This is because weather patterns, adjacent mountains and distance from moist ocean air all combine in this part of North America to create the very dry conditions typical of desert areas. But why have these areas been divided into four separate deserts? What makes them different?

Bark Scorpion

Botanists (scientists who study plants) looked at the many different plants that grow in the desert areas. They noticed that certain plants were very common in some areas and uncommon in other areas. Zoologists (scientists who study animals) found the same thing was true about some of the animals. Scientists also looked at things like temperature, elevation, average amount of available moisture and the season during which it usually rains. When they put all of this information together, they were able to identify four major desert areas that were different from each other.

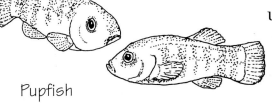

Pupfish

This book has information on each of the North American desert regions. In addition, Death Valley (part of the Mojave Desert) and the Colorado Desert (part of the Sonoran Desert) have been included as separate sections because of special animals, plants or other features that make them unique. Drawings of the deserts show the plants and animals in the types of places you might find them if you visit. The nocturnal animals are under the night sky.

The desert is a very special place. Use this book to help you explore some of the secrets that are waiting to be discovered.

Many plants and animals of the desert are found in specific habitat areas. This is because

Prickly-pear Cactus

their needs are different. For example, the **desert tortoise** and the **kangaroo rat** build underground homes, so they need to live where the ground is soft enough to dig their burrows, such as near washes. **Fan palms** need to always have their roots in water, so they only grow in riparian areas with year-round water like springs.

Sometimes animals make use of more than one habitat area. **Bighorn sheep** prefer the steep, rocky hillsides and cliffs but also need to drink water. So they never live too far from riparian areas. **Kit foxes** may stay among the rocks of the upper bajada during the day, but will go to a wash at night to hunt and eat the rodents that dig their burrows there. These two pages show a cross-section of several desert habitats with examples of the plants and animals that might live there.

A **wash** is a riverbed that has running water when it rains, but is often dry. **Ironwood** and **smoke trees** grow along washes and small rodents dig their burrows into the sand along the edges.

A shallow, low lying area that water drains into after a rain is called a **playa.** Sometimes this rain creates a shallow lake, but the water evaporates quickly, and the playa is dry most of the time. It can also be a salty place, because the rainwater washes salts out of the surrounding hills and mountains, and these are left behind when the rainwater evaporates. When that happens, only plants that can tolerate high concentrations of salt, such as **pickleweed**, can grow there.

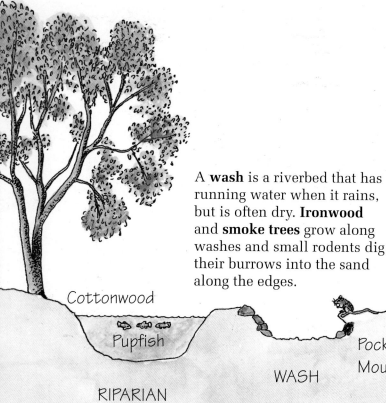

Cottonwood

Pupfish

RIPARIAN

WASH

Pocket
Mouse

Pickleweed

PLAYA

Mesquite

DUNES

Riparian areas, such as ponds or streams, have water all year long. **Cottonwood** trees grow in wet areas and many of the birds and larger mammals that need year-round water are found in, or close to, riparian habitats.

Then there are the **dunes.** These are shifting hills made up of either sand (a mixture of various minerals) or white gypsum (pure silica). **Mesquite** and the **Jerusalem cricket** are among the few plants and animals that make their home there.

The **sky** is a place to see many animals of the desert, although it is not a true habitat. During the day, look for hawks, butterflies and bees. At night, bats, owls and moths are sometimes seen.

The rocky **hillsides** and **mountains** often have cooler temperatures, and some animals go there to escape the heat from the desert floor. Other animals, like the **bighorn sheep**, prefer the steep hillside areas and are found there most of the time.

Bighorn Sheep

Owls and Hawks

Bats

Harris' Hawk

Saguaro

Barrel Cactus

Painted Lady

Pronghorn

Coyote

UPPER BAJADA

Creosote

Woodrat Nest

Joshua Tree

MIDDLE BAJADA

Beavertail Cactus

Cottontail

LOWER BAJADA

Yucca

Along the base of many desert hills and mountains is the **bajada.** This is an area of sand, gravel and small rocks that have washed out of the nearby mountains, forming a gentle slope. Many plants and animals live on the bajada. **Cacti**, **Joshua trees** and **creosote bushes** are common on bajadas, and many insects, small mammals and birds can be found in and around the plants growing on the lower, middle or upper bajada slopes.

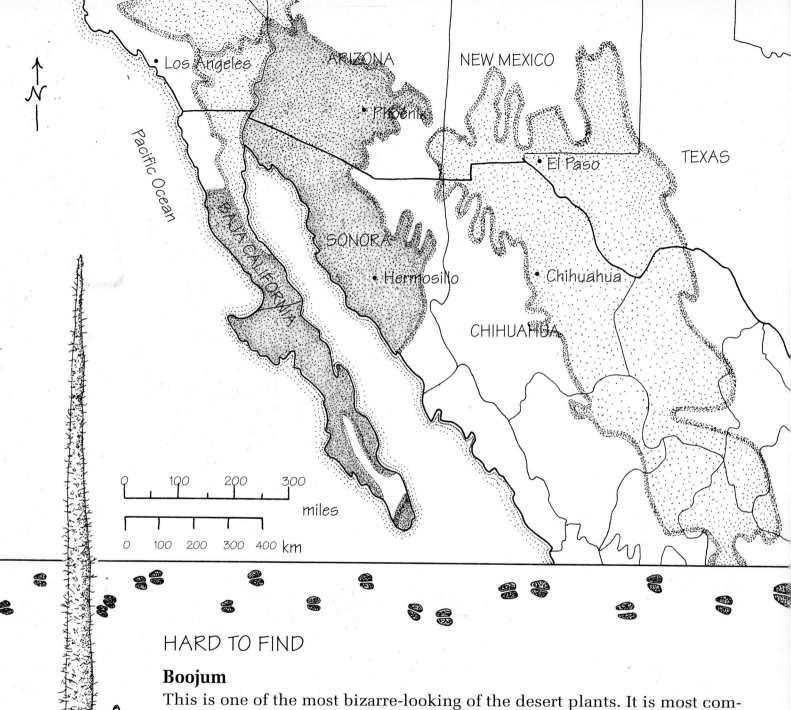

Los Angeles

ARIZONA

NEW MEXICO

Phoenix

Pacific Ocean

El Paso

TEXAS

BAJA CALIFORNIA

SONORA

Hermosillo

Chihuahua

CHIHUAHUA

0   100   200   300
miles

0   100   200   300   400   km

HARD TO FIND

Boojum

This is one of the most bizarre-looking of the desert plants. It is most commonly found in and near Baja California, in the Sonoran Desert area. It is slow-growing and can be up to 70 feet (21 m) tall! Also called cirio ("candle" in Spanish), it was named boojum after a "mythical thing found in desolate faraway lands" from the poem *The Hunting of the Snark* by Lewis Carroll.

Sonoran Desert

One of the most popular and well-known deserts is the Sonoran. Named after the Mexican state of Sonora, it has more types of plants than any of the other North American deserts. This is due partly to its two seasons of rain: winter rain from the Pacific Ocean, and summer rain from the Gulf of Mexico. The Sonoran Desert is also one of the hottest deserts. Summer temperatures can reach over 120°F (49°C), and winter temperatures rarely get below freezing.

The Sonoran Desert is the home of the huge **saguaro**, a cactus that can be up to 50 feet (15 m) tall and over 150 years old. Many animals live in and around the **saguaro**: **Gila woodpeckers**, **elf owls**, **Harris' hawks**, lizards and **woodrats**. And the summer fruit of the **saguaro** provides food not only for animals, but for people, too. Native Americans have used the fruit for years, eating it fresh or making it into cakes or syrup.

The poisonous **Gila monster**, one of only two poisonous lizards in the world, also lives in the Sonoran desert. The poison comes out through grooves in its teeth, and it kills its prey by biting down and grinding its jaws.

Gila Monster

It is black and reddish-pink, and about 1½ feet (0.5 m) long, but it's rarely seen in the wild.

The **cardón**, perhaps the largest cactus in the world, is from the southern Sonoran Desert. Its trunk can be 3 feet (1 m) wide and 6 feet (1.8 m) high. From there its branches may reach up 40 feet or more.

And would you think that sea turtles and gulls live in the desert? Well, they do … in a part of the Sonoran Desert that borders the sea.

No American desert is quite like this one. With so many different things to try to see, you'll have to come back again and again.

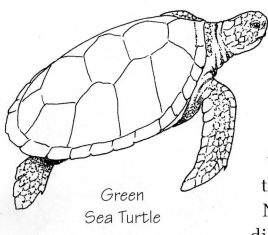

Green
Sea Turtle

SONORAN DESERT

Turkey Vulture

Harris' Hawk

Gila Woodpecker

Creosote

Palo Verde

Young Saguaro

Teddy-bear Cholla

Organ Pipe Cactus

Cactus Wren

Chain-fruit Cholla

Coati

Gambel's Quail

Mexican Poppy

Collared Lizard

Greater Roadrunner

Brittlebush

Velvet Ant

Tarantula

Western Whiptail

12 Side-blotched Lizard

Bat

Cottonwood

Soaptree
Yucca

Mule Deer

Cougar

Ocotillo

Black-tailed
Jackrabbit

Kingsnake

Cardón

Rattlesnake

Ringtail Cat

Prickly-pear
Cactus

Javelina

Woodrat and
Nest

Cottontail
Rabbit

Bark Scorpion

Owl's-clover

Stink Beetle

13

HARD TO FIND

Sand Food

This is a desert parasite. It looks a little bit like a large mushroom partly buried in the sand. There are light purple flowers in a circle on its 5-inch (12.7 cm) diameter top. The underground stalk was used by Native Americans for food. It is found in sandy areas.

Colorado Desert (Sonoran Desert)

The winter rains of this desert change areas of dry desert plants to colorful fields of yellow, red and orange flowers. Water trickles over rocks, and quail gather under the shade of tall palm trees. Part of the Sonoran Desert, the Colorado Desert gets its name from the Colorado River, which flows between California and Arizona. Although it does not have the variety of the greater Sonoran Desert, many special things are found here.

Elephant Tree

In canyons, along deep cracks in the earth that allow water to rise to the surface, are the **fan palm** oases. These are areas of natural water and shade that attract many kinds of desert animals including **Gambel's quail** and **bighorn sheep**. Almost all **fan palms** are found in the Colorado Desert.

A hiking trail in Anza-Borrego State Park leads you to one of the most bizarre desert plants, the **elephant tree**. This short, fat plant looks like it has the legs of a purplish elephant (if you use your imagination). It occurs in the Colorado Desert, and only in a few hidden areas.

One of the largest desert sand dune areas in North America is here: the Algodones Dunes. These dunes are about 4–8 miles (6.4–12.8 km) wide and 45 miles (72.4 km) long! To survive in a sand dune area, many plants have very long roots, which help anchor them to the sand and bring water from far beneath the sand's surface.

Fish-hook Cactus

Cacti grow here too. Look for the **fish-hook cactus**. It's not very big—about 6 inches (15 cm) tall—but it has large, dark-colored spines that stick out of it and hook down at the end … like fishhooks.

This desert is really fun to visit. A hike along a canyon stream with a picnic under the palm trees is a great way to see some of the many plants and animals that live here. But don't forget to visit the rocky hillsides and hidden valleys. Pack plenty of water, and put on your hat and hiking shoes for a great time.

COLORADO DESERT

Bighorn Sheep

Red-tailed Hawk

Cottonwood

Pencil Cholla

Ocotillo

Barrel Cactus

Mojave Yucca

Cactus Wren

Smoke Tree

Hedgehog Cactus

Silver Cholla

Desert Spiny Lizard

Sidewinder

Costa's Hummingbird

Chuparosa

Antelope Squirrel

Indigo Bush

Mormon Tea

Desert Dandelion

Painted Lady

Greater Roadrunner

Sand Verbena

Chuckwalla

Ironwood

Bat

Fan Palm

White-lined
Sphinx Moth

Coyote

Creosote
Bush

Agave

Black-tailed
Jackrabbit

Teddy-bear
Cholla

Brittlebush

Beavertail
Cactus

Kangaroo Rat

Pocket Mouse

Collared
Lizard

Fish-hook
Cactus

Gambel's Quail

Evening Primrose

Arizona Blister Beetle

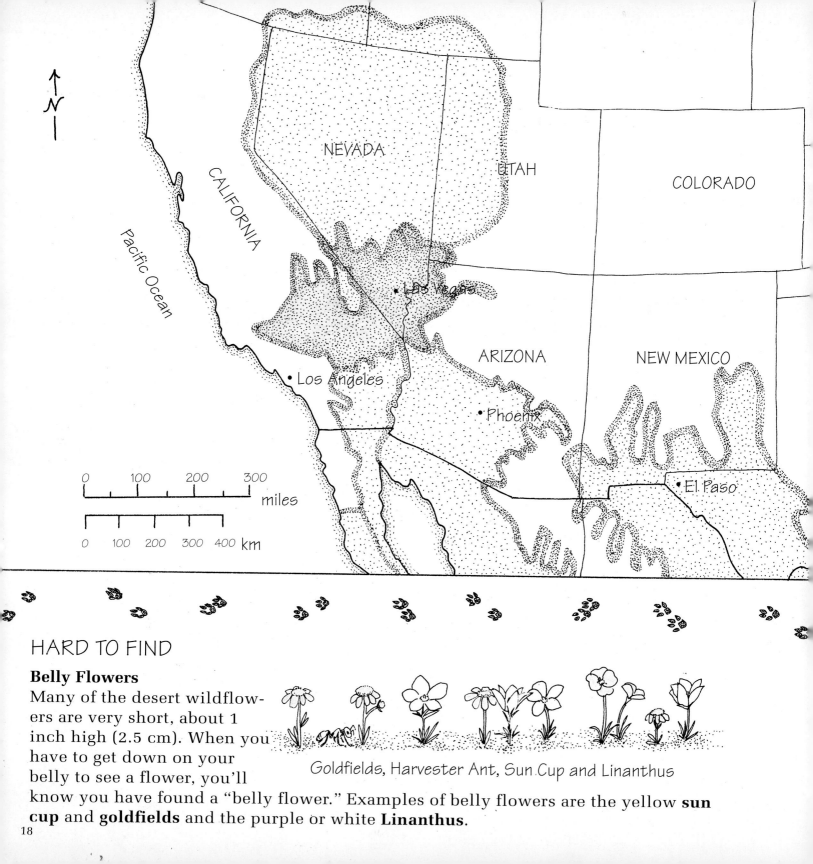

HARD TO FIND

Belly Flowers

Many of the desert wildflowers are very short, about 1 inch high (2.5 cm). When you have to get down on your belly to see a flower, you'll

Goldfields, Harvester Ant, Sun Cup and Linanthus

know you have found a "belly flower." Examples of belly flowers are the yellow **sun cup** and **goldfields** and the purple or white **Linanthus.**

Mojave Desert

About a one-hour drive from Los Angeles, California, is the area known as the Mojave, the smallest of the North American deserts. It is called a high desert because its elevation averages from about 3,000 feet (900 m) to 5,500 feet (1,700 m) above sea level. Mountains to the south and west prevent most rainclouds from getting to the Mojave Desert, and the average winter rainfall is only 5–8 inches (12.5–20 cm). Summers are hot and dry with temperatures averaging about 105°F (41°C).

Sometimes in the spring, wildflowers cover hillsides with colors of orange, yellow and purple. Some of these spring plants provide food for the **desert tortoise**, an endangered desert animal. These reptiles live underground in burrows throughout the cold Mojave Desert winter and are most often seen walking around in the spring when the days are warming up.

Winters in the Mojave Desert can get very cold, and snow is not uncommon. This is one reason why much of this desert is covered in shrubs instead of cacti. **Creosote bushes**, found in all of the hot deserts of North America, are very common here. Look around them for insects like the **desert spider beetle**, a type of **blister beetle**. Some of these beetles contain a liquid that can cause blisters on some people, so be careful around them.

Desert Spider Beetle

The most bizarre plant of the Mojave Desert is probably the **Joshua tree**. It is a tall, spiny yucca that is very common, but found almost solely in the Mojave Desert. Many animals are found around **Joshua trees**. Look for the orange and

Desert Night Lizard

black **Scott's oriole** and the **ladder-backed woodpecker**. If you carefully move a dead **Joshua tree** branch off the ground (use a stick, in case a snake is resting under the branch), you might even see the tiny speckled **desert night lizard**. (Be sure to put the branch back carefully.)

There are also caves and sand dunes to visit in this desert. Guided tours lead you through Mitchell Caverns where it's always 65°F (18°C) and the Kelso Sand Dunes make rumbling or booming noises when you walk on them (really!). Enjoy the Mojave Desert. It's a great place with lots to see and explore.

MOJAVE DESERT

Yucca Moth

Red-tailed Hawk

Raven

Phainopepla

Scott's Oriole

Cactus Wren and Nest

Mesquite

Ladder-backed Woodpecker

Joshua Tree

Desert Willow

Teddy-bear Cholla

Antelope Squirrel

Claret Cup Cactus

Patchnose Snake

Lupine

Desert Tortoise

Chuckwalla

California Poppy

Gambel's Quail

Desert Spiny Lizard

Velvet Ant

Side-blotched Lizard

Goldfields

Bighorn Sheep

Bat

White-lined Sphinx Moth

Barrel Cactus

Coyote

Mojave Yucca

Bobcat

Antillean Blue Butterfly

Creosote Bush

Coyote Melon

Silver Cholla

Greater Roadrunner

Brittlebush

Black-tailed Jackrabbit

Kit Fox

Desert Hairy Scorpion

Cottontail Rabbit

Pocket Mouse

Kangaroo Rat

BeavertailCactus

Woodrat and Nest

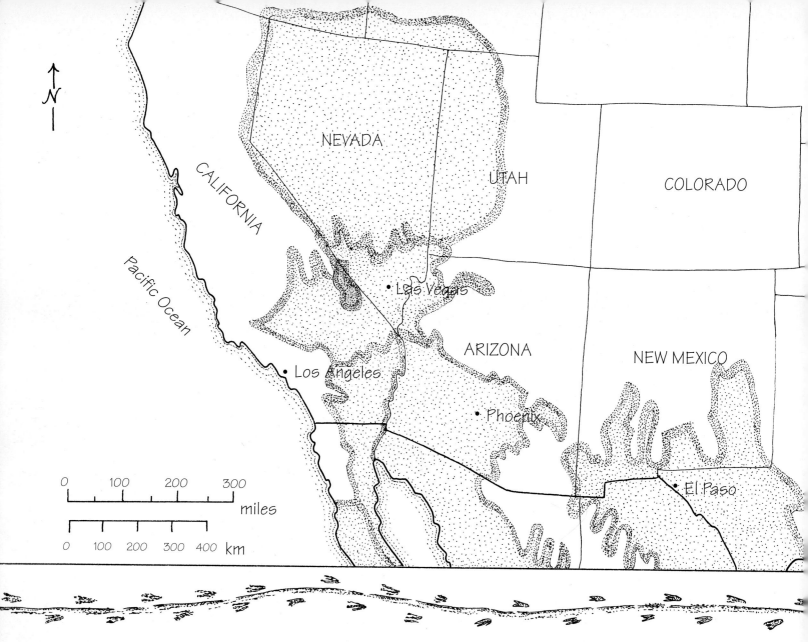

HARD TO FIND

Antlion or Doodlebug

Pretend you're an ant. You're walking along the edge of a small pit in the sand, when suddenly the ground beneath your feet starts to slip away, and you slide down into the jaws of a hideous-looking creature waiting to eat you at the bottom. Fortunately for people, young antlions or doodlebugs are really small, less than ¹/₄ inch (0.6 cm) long and only eat ants or other small insects.

Death Valley (Mojave Desert)

Death Valley is located in the northern part of the Mojave Desert. It was given its name by a group of travelers who wandered into the area around 1850 and almost died there.

This small desert area is almost surrounded by mountains, including the very high Sierra Nevada to the west. Rainclouds moving eastward drop most of their moisture onto these mountains and very little moisture into Death Valley. The average rainfall is less than 2 inches (5 cm) per year. Most of the water that finally does make it into Death Valley evaporates into the air. Salts washed out of the surrounding mountains from the rain and melting snow end up on the surface of the valley floor. Over thousands of years, this has created pools of salty water and dry salt flats covering an area of over 200 square miles (518 square km). Yet, a thousand different plants and hundreds of different kinds of animals live in this desert environment. The common **saltbush** and **pickleweed** grow in soil too salty for most other plants. You may find them at the edge of pools and streams that contain the **pupfish**, a tiny, silvery fish that can live in

Desert-sunflower

water as salty as the ocean. Along the sides of the road, you may see the bright yellow **desert-sunflower**, the pinkish **desert five-spot** or the white **rock nettle**.

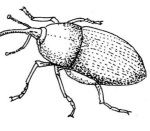

Snout Beetle

The animals may be harder to find. Look for insects like the **snout beetle** in the bushes or on the flowers and reptiles like the **side-blotched lizard** among the rocks. Visit areas that have water in the morning or early evening and you're sure to see some birds and maybe larger animals coming for a drink.

Death Valley is also known for things other than its plants and animals, such as its temperature, which was the hottest ever recorded in North America: 134°F (57°C) at Furnace Creek. Summer temperatures commonly reach about 120°F (49°C)! It also has the lowest place on land in all of North America: 282 feet (86 m) *below* sea level on the salt flats near a place called Badwater.

Death Valley is an incredible place. Wear your shade hat, pack your water bottle and be prepared for an adventure.

DEATH VALLEY

Turkey Vulture

Cottonwood

Creosote Bush

Globemallow

Beavertail Cactus

Mojave-aster

Coachwhip

Antelope
Squirrel

Greater
Roadrunner

Evening
Primrose

Desert
Holly

Pickleweed

Tarantula
Hawk

Mourning
Dove

Tarantula

Side-blotched
Lizard

Desert
Five-spot

Desert Gold

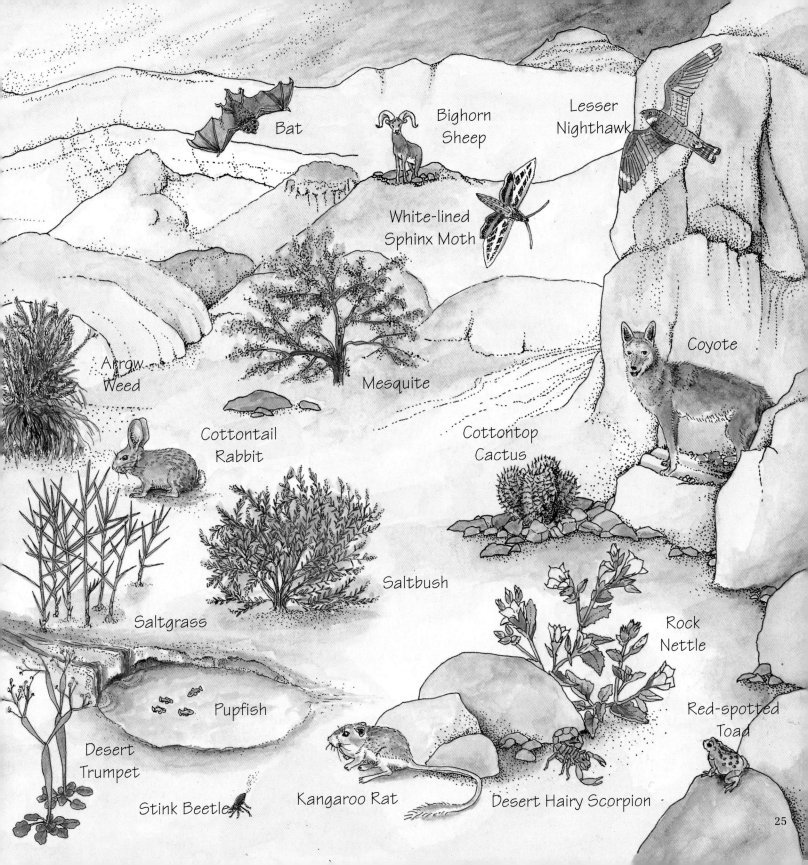

Bat

Bighorn
Sheep

Lesser
Nighthawk

White-lined
Sphinx Moth

Arrow
Weed

Mesquite

Coyote

Cottontail
Rabbit

Cottontop
Cactus

Saltbush

Saltgrass

Rock
Nettle

Pupfish

Red-spotted
Toad

Desert
Trumpet

Stink Beetle

Kangaroo Rat

Desert Hairy Scorpion

25

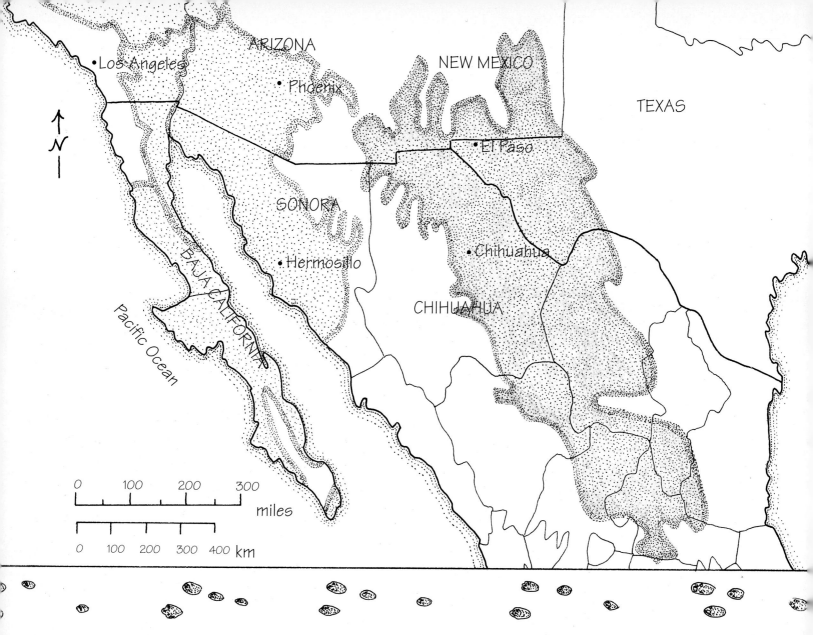

HARD TO FIND

Horned Lizards

When these spiny lizards stay very still, they blend in
with the background and are very hard to spot.
They look sort of fat (from eating mostly ants,
their favorite food) and are sometimes called
horned "toads." They also do a really weird thing: If
they are caught, they can squirt blood from their eyelids!

Chihuahuan Desert

The largest desert is the Chihuahuan, making up about $\frac{1}{3}$ (35%) of the total desert area in North America. Most of this desert extends onto the Mexican plateau, an area of high elevation. As a result, about one-half of the Chihuahuan Desert is above 4,000 feet (1,220 m). This desert gets rain mostly during summer thunderstorms, with moisture coming from the Gulf of Mexico. The result is that the plants have flowers in the fall. The amount of rainfall throughout the desert varies from 3 inches (7.6 cm) to about 16 inches (40.6 cm). Summer temperatures can get up to about 90°F (32°C), and winter temperatures can go below freezing, mostly in the higher elevations.

Camel Cricket

The Chihuahuan Desert has one of the most beautiful "sand dune" areas of all the North American deserts: the gypsum dunes of southern New Mexico. These dunes are not the light golden-brown of the other sand dunes. Instead, they are almost pure white, made up of a variety of gypsum called selenite that washes out of the nearby mountains. And even here, among these snow-white dunes, some plants and animals have made their home. Look for the **soaptree yucca**, **camel cricket** and the light-colored **bleached earless lizard**.

Farther south, the land is made up of high, flat areas of sand and gravel. **Creosote bushes** are very common here, along with more **soaptree yucca** and **honey mesquite**. Look for **tree chollas** and **cactus wrens** with their nests in the cholla branches. There are **agaves** like the **lechuguilla** (which means "little lettuce" in Spanish) on the sides of mountains and cacti like the **barrel cactus** on the rocky bajadas. Also, lots of grasses grow in the high, cooler areas of the Chihuahuan Desert.

Soaptree Yucca

Animals to look for throughout the Chihuahuan Desert are **ravens**, **horned larks**, **bats**, **jackrabbits**, **cottontail rabbits**, **ants**, **beetles** and **scorpions**.

Horned Lark

Wow! This desert sure has a lot of stuff to see. But watch out for those summer rains. Better keep your hat on for protection against the sun *and* the rain.

Harris' Hawk

Creosote Bush

Ocotillo

Bighorn Sheep

Indian Ricegrass

Claret Cup Cactus

Tree Cholla

Ladder-backed Woodpecker

Sotol

Agave

Mormon Tea

Lupine

Greater Roadrunner

Scaled Quail

Mexican Poppy

Javelina

Prickly-pear Cactus

Mourning Dove

Rattlesnake

Bat

Mesquite

Pyrrhuloxia

Nevada
Buck-moth

Coyote

Yucca
Moth

Banana
Yucca

Lechuguilla

Soaptree
Yucca

Prince's
Plume

Kit Fox

Black-tailed
Jackrabbit

Burrowing
Owl

Kangaroo
Rat

Desert Hairy
Scorpion

Stink Beetle

Sand Verbena

Jerusalem
Cricket

Centipede

29

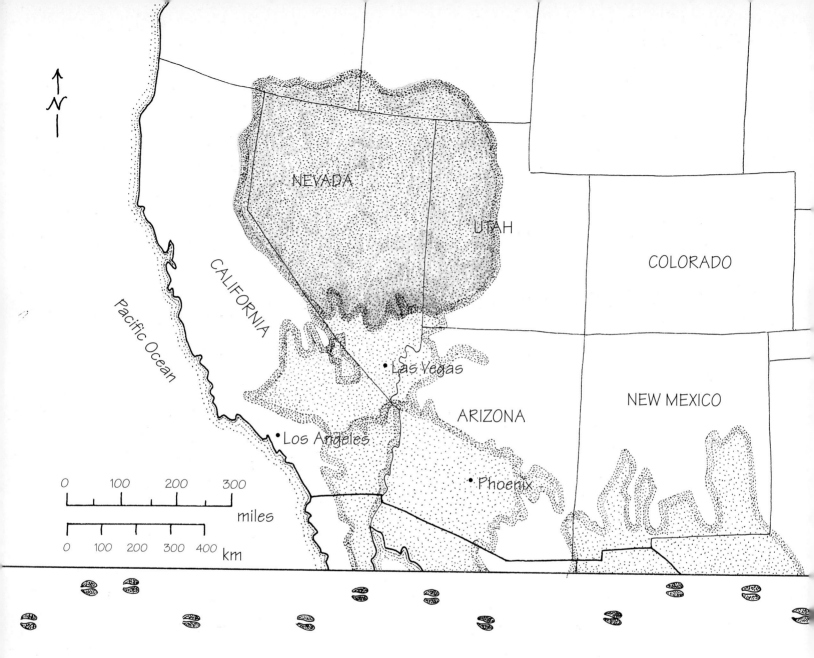

NEVADA

UTAH

CALIFORNIA

COLORADO

Pacific Ocean

•Las Vegas

NEW MEXICO

ARIZONA

•Los Angeles

0   100   200   300
miles

•Phoenix

0   100   200   300   400   km

HARD TO FIND

Spadefoot Toad

These toads stay underground in burrows when the ground
is dry. Look for them in sandy or gravelly areas after it has
rained, especially in the Chihuahuan and Great Basin
deserts. They're only about 2 inches (5 cm) long.

Great Basin Desert

The northernmost Great Basin Desert is a cold desert. (Cold? A desert that's cold?) The Great Basin is a high desert with 5,000-foot (1,525 m) valleys and mountains over 13,000 feet (4,000 m) in elevation. Its average yearly rainfall is under 10 inches (25 cm), just like most deserts, but summer temperatures are not as hot, and winter temperatures are often below freezing. Much of the winter rain comes down as snow. This affects the plants and animals that live there in two ways. First, they have to be able to survive freezing temperatures for a long time. You won't see many plants like cacti which can freeze and die in the snow. Second, the plants get most of their water in spring, when the snow melts. This means that the growing season is very short, followed quickly by the dry summer. Plants like annual wildflowers are not very abundant because they don't have much time to sprout, flower and set seeds for the following year.

The most common plants in the Great Basin Desert are shrubs. One of the most common shrubs is called **big sagebrush**, and its flower is the state flower of Nevada. (Look closely, and you'll see that **big sagebrush** has leaves that look like long, skinny duck feet.) If you look around the shrubs, you'll see grasses, some annual wildflowers and other smaller shrubs. And don't forget to look for signs of animals. Because

Sage Grouse   Big Sagebrush

Skunk

there are so many bushes, it's sometimes hard to see animals like **jackrabbits** and **ground squirrels** and birds like the **sage grouse**, but they're there somewhere. You may even see one of the fastest animals of North America in the distance, the **pronghorn antelope**.

The mountains of this desert have fir, spruce and pine trees, including the **bristlecone pines**, among the oldest living things on Earth. The animals of the mountains include deer, **marmots** and **skunks**.

The Great Basin Desert is very big. With its shrubs, trees and abundant wildlife, there is much to see. But don't forget: It's a cold desert, and you may need your jacket when you explore it.

GREAT BASIN DESERT

Golden Eagle

Ponderosa Pine

Marmot

Raven

Juniper

Mule Deer

Piñon Pine

Skunk

Globemallow

Rattlesnake

Porcupine

Prickly-pear
Cactus

Lupine

Antelope
Squirrel

Prickly
Poppy

Side-blotched
Lizard

Monkeyflower

Bat

Pronghorn

Coyote

Rabbit Brush

Yucca

Black-tailed
Jackrabbit

Mormon
Tea

Big
Sagebrush

Prince's
Plume

Shad-scale

Sage Grouse

Kangaroo Rat

Indian Paintbrush

Desert
Trumpet

Cottontail
Rabbit

Pocket
Mouse

Common Plants and Animals

Some plants and animals are so common they occur in two or more deserts. **Bats** and **coyotes**, for example, occur in all of the desert areas. This does not mean that you will see all of these animals each time you visit a desert, but the chances are pretty good that you'll see one or more of them.

Information next to the drawings will help you learn where to look and what to look for. Remember that the time of year and the time of day you go looking for things are important, too. The annual wildflowers will be growing for only a few weeks after the rainy season, and most of the animals will not be out in the middle of a hot day.

While exploring the desert, keep in mind that some plants and animals can hurt you or make you sick if they touch your skin or mouth. You may want to gently touch a cactus spine or leaf to look at it more closely, but be sure to wash your hands very well afterwards.

Learn to look carefully and listen well. You may be surprised to discover things you never knew were there.

BAT
Color: Brown.
Size: Body is about 3–4 inches (7.6–10.2 cm) long.
Food: Insects or nectar from flowers.
Notes: Looking like weird, brown birds, bats are actually furry mammals. Look for them after sunset fluttering in the sky or scooping up water from a desert pool.

COYOTE
Color: Light brown, gray and white.
Size: About the size of a large dog, 3–4 feet (1–1.2 m) long.
Food: Omnivorous, eating almost anything.
Notes: Blends in well with the desert sand and rocks. Its "yipping" call can sometimes be heard on the desert at night. Coyotes are sometimes seen during the day, but usually come out at night, having spent the day in underground burrows.

PAINTED LADY BUTTERFLY

Color: Light orange with white spots over black wing edges.
Size: About 2 inches (5 cm).
Food: Flower nectar, especially **lupine**.
Notes: This butterfly is found in more parts of the world than any other butterfly.

JACKRABBIT

Color: Grayish tan and white.
Size: 18–25 inches (about 0.5 m)
Food: Plants.
Notes: Huge ears and a thin, light-colored body make it easy to identify a jackrabbit. This very common nocturnal animal is found in all of the North American deserts. Look for it in the light from car headlights, sitting or running along roads at night.

SNAKES

Color: Lots of different colors, but usually with some brown or tan.
Size: About 1–7 feet (0.3–2.1 m), depending on the kind of snake it is.
Food: Rodents, lizards and other small animals.
Notes: Even though many people think there are only poisonous rattlesnakes in the deserts, there are lots of other snakes, too. The super-fast, long and thin **coachwhip** is one that is out during the day. Sometimes reddish in color, it can climb bushes and trees to look for food or to escape being caught.

TAMARISK

Color: Green leaves, pink flowers in the spring.
Size: 16 feet (4.9 m) tall.
Notes: This very common bushy tree is most often found in riparian habitats and along major roads. Tamarisk was brought from Europe and Asia many years ago as a new plant for desert areas. It spread really fast, crowding out the original desert plants. Tamarisks are now being removed in many areas so that native desert plants can grow back.

Birds

COSTA'S HUMMINGBIRD
Color: Purplish on the top of the head and on the face. The body is greenish on the back and white on the belly.
Size: 3–4 inches (7.6–10 cm).
Food: Flower nectar (usually from red flowers), insects and spiders.
Notes: A very small and fast-flying bird, look for them around red flowers.

RED-TAILED HAWK
Color: Body is light tan on bottom, brown on top; reddish brown tail is visible when the hawk turns as it soars.
Size: 19–25 inches (48–64 cm).
Food: Rodents, rabbits and some reptiles.
Notes: Look for it circling in the sky during the day.

GAMBEL'S QUAIL
Color: Male is brownish gray above, whitish on the bottom and has a black patch on the belly. He has a black face and a bunch of feathers sticking out of the top of the head. The female is a little plainer.
Size: 10–12 inches (25–30.5 cm).
Food: Insects, seeds and berries.
Notes: Usually found near water and bushes, often with other **Gambel's quail**.

RAVEN
Color: All black.
Size: 21–27 inches (53–69 cm).
Food: Omnivorous (this means it eats practically everything: seeds, fruit, insects, sandwiches left after a picnic, etc.)
Notes: Look for the **raven** either flying in the sky or on the top of a tree or large bush.

CACTUS WREN
Color: Light tan with small dark spots all over the body.
Size: 7–9 inches (17.8–22.9 cm).
Food: Insects and spiders.
Notes: Look for nests in cholla; the nests are sort of the shape of a football, but more rounded with a hole on the side. The state bird of Arizona is the **cactus wren**.

MOURNING DOVE
Color: Light brownish gray.
Size: 11–13 inches (28–33 cm).
Food: Seeds and insects.
Notes: A very common bird often seen walking or at rest near water.

ROADRUNNER
Color: Blotchy brown above, streaked brown on white below.
Size: 20–24 inches (50.8–61 cm).
Food: Insects and reptiles.
Notes: Often seen running along open areas of sand or small gravel, such as along a road. This is the state bird of New Mexico.

Arthropods (Insects and Their Relatives)

ANTS

Color: Any color from red to brown to black.
Size: Small.
Food: Some of the most common ants of the desert are **harvester ants** who collect seeds.
Notes: Look for volcano-shaped mounds leading into their tunnels in areas of sand or fine gravel. Beware the red ants … they can bite and sting.

STINK BEETLES

Color: Black.
Size: 1–1¹/₂ inches (2.5–3.8 cm).
Food: Plant material.
Notes: When disturbed, these beetles will stick their rear into the air and may release a smelly liquid. They're also called **pinacate** or **circus beetles**. Look for them slowly walking about in the early evening and at night.

VELVET ANTS

Color: White, yellow, orange, red and/or black.
Size: About 1 inch (2.5 cm).
Food: Nectar of flowers.
Notes: These fuzzy ant-looking insects are really a type of wingless female wasp. They can give you a painful sting. Do not pick them up! They are sometimes seen crawling along open areas like roadsides.

DESERT HAIRY SCORPION

Color: Black and pale yellowish tan.
Size: 5¹/₂ inches (14 cm).
Food: Insects and maybe small lizards.
Notes: They are nocturnal and can sting, but do not usually attack people. Try to find them at night with a "black light."

WHITE-LINED SPHINX MOTH

Color: Tan and black with white and pink stripes.
Size: Wingspan about 3 inches (7.5 cm).
Food: Flower nectar.
Notes: They are nocturnal and are sometimes seen around artificial lights at night.

TARANTULA

Color: Brown or black.
Size: Body 2–2¹/₂ inches long (5–6.4 cm).
Food: Insects and sometimes small lizards.
Notes: A fairly shy spider, they are usually seen crawling around at night.

TARANTULA HAWK WASP

Color: Blue-black body and orange-yellow wings.
Size: About 1¹/₂ inches (3.8 cm).
Food: Adults drink flower nectar. Young eat paralyzed tarantulas.
Notes: These wasps will sting and paralyze a tarantula, drag

it into an underground burrow, and lay eggs on the tarantula's body so the young wasps will have something to eat when they hatch out.

Mammals

COTTONTAIL RABBIT
Color: Light brown with a white tail.

Size: 14 inches (35.6 cm).

Food: Plants, like grasses and leaves.

Notes: A nocturnal animal, the **cottontail rabbit** may also be out in the very early morning or late afternoon. Look for it near bushes and rocks where it hides.

MICE and RATS
Color: Mostly shades of brown or gray. **Kangaroo rats** are white and golden tan.

Size: From the 4-inch- (10 cm) long **pocket mouse** to the 15-inch- (38.1 cm) long **woodrat**.

Food: Plant material like seeds and fruit, and insects and other arthropods.

Notes: These animals live in rocky and/or sandy areas, usually spending the day in burrows. The **woodrat** piles cactus pieces, leaves and sticks at the entrance to its burrow. Look for **woodrat** nests at the base of large cacti or bushes or in rocky areas.

JAVELINA or COLLARED PECCARY
Color: Dark gray with a light-colored band, like a collar, on the shoulder area.

Size: About 3 feet (1 m).

Food: Mainly cactus, especially **prickly-pear cactus**.

Notes: Peccaries are active during the day, except when it is really hot. They are usually found in groups.

KIT FOX
Color: Very light tan.

Size: Body length about 20 inches (0.5 m).

Food: Small rodents like **kangaroo rats**, lizards and insects.

Notes: Kit foxes are mainly nocturnal and can be seen near sandy areas. Look for their tracks near rodent burrows in the early morning.

BIGHORN SHEEP
Color: Light tan.

Size: Body length is 4–6 feet (1.2–1.8 m).

Food: Plants.

Notes: Look for these hard to see animals during the day on cliff faces and on rocky hillsides near year-round water. Listen for the sound of rocks and gravel loosened and sliding down a hill...it may be some **bighorn sheep** moving up the hillside.

PRONGHORN
Color: White and dark tan.

Size: 4–4½ feet (1.2–1.4 m).

Food: Sagebrush, grasses, and other plants and their leaves.

Notes: Look for the **pronghorn** across open areas. They are the fastest-running animal in North America.

ANTELOPE SQUIRREL
Color: Brownish with a white stripe down each side of its body.

Size: Body length about 8–9 inches (20–22.9 cm).

Food: Seeds and fruit.

Notes: Gets most of its water from the food it eats. Active during the day in the desert foothills.

CHUCKWALLA

Color: Brown, gray and/or black.

Size: Up to about 18 inches (45.7 cm).

Food: Plants.

Notes: This herbivore does not drink water. It gets all the water it needs from the plants it eats. It also has a great way of protecting itself: If some other animal is trying to get the **chuckwalla**, it slips between some rocks and "puffs" up its body so that it can't be pulled out. Look for them during the day in rocky areas.

RATTLESNAKE

Color: Light tan to dark grayish brown. May have diamond-shaped pattern on its back.

Size: 18 inches (45.7 cm) (**sidewinder**) to about 7 feet (2.1 m) (western diamondback).

Food: Mostly rodents, like mice and rats.

Notes: Rattlesnakes are often out late in the afternoon, but can be found at all times of the day. The **sidewinder** makes an "S" shaped track when it moves across the desert sand. All **rattlesnakes,** even babies, can bite and are **poisonous**. Do not go near them.

SIDE-BLOTCHED LIZARD

Color: Light brown. May have light blue color and/or bands along tail.

Size: Up to 6 inches (15.2 cm).

Food: Insects.

Notes: A really common desert lizard that is often out during the day, even when it's very hot.

DESERT SPINY LIZARD

Color: Brown or yellowish brown, sometimes with blue under the head and on the sides of the belly area.

Size: About 4–9 inches (10.2–22.9 cm).

Food: Insects and other lizards.

Notes: This lizard is seen during the day on rocks, in trees and on the ground.

COLLARED LIZARD

Color: Yellowish brown or yellowish blue with a black and white band around the back of its neck.

Size: 8–14 inches (20.3–35.6 cm).

Food: Insects and small lizards.

Notes: Look for them in rocky areas sunning themselves in the early-morning sun. They will bite, so be very careful.

DESERT TORTOISE

Color: Brown.

Size: Up to about 14 inches (35.6 cm).

Food: Plants.

Notes: Look for this herbivore in areas of sand or soft dirt where it digs burrows to escape the hottest part of the day. It also stays underground all winter, when it's cold. This tortoise is endangered and is also the state reptile of California.

Annual Wildflowers

EVENING PRIMROSE
Color: White flowers, dark green leaves.
Size: Up to 1 foot (30 cm) tall.
Notes: The flowers open up in the late afternoon and early evening and are pollinated by the **white-lined sphinx moth**.

CALIFORNIA and MEXICAN POPPY
Color: Orange flowers with almost grayish green leaves.
Size: Up to about 1½ feet (50 cm).
Notes: One of the few orange flowers of the desert. Look for them spread across gentle slopes and hillsides. (The **California poppy** is the state flower of California.)

PHACELIA
Color: Light purple to dark purple flowers and green leaves.
Size: Up to about 1 foot (30 cm) tall.
Notes: A common purple wildflower often seen on roadsides, in washes and on bajadas.

JIMSON WEED
Color: White flowers, dark green leaves.
Size: Up to 3 feet (1 m) tall.
Notes: As its name implies, this is a "weed" and non-native that grows in many dry areas of North America. It forms big clumps of leaves and flowers and is commonly found along roads.

SAND VERBENA
Color: Pink flower clusters on green stems and leaves.
Size: About 10 inches (25 cm) tall, with viney stems growing out about 3 feet (1 m) from the center.
Notes: This plant can color huge sandy areas pink in the springtime.

LUPINE
Color: Bluish purple to pinkish purple flowers with green leaves.
Size: About 1 foot (30 cm) tall.
Notes: Look for lupines along roadsides and open, flat desert areas. They have really distinct leaves that are easy to identify. The state flower of Texas is a **lupine**.

OWL'S-CLOVER
Color: Purplish pink flowers with light green leaves.
Size: Up to about 1 foot (30 cm) tall.
Notes: The flower clusters at the top of this plant are soft because of short "hairs" that cover the flower parts. Look for **owl's-clover** in open, flat areas where it sometimes covers the ground with its purplish pink color.

Cacti

BEAVERTAIL CACTUS
Color: Gray green pads and bright pinkish red flowers in the spring.
Size: About 1 foot (30 cm) tall.
Notes: The spines on this cactus are short, bunched together, and look like fuzzy spots. They can stay stuck in your fingers if you touch them, so be careful. Look for this cactus in fairly flat areas, sometimes between other bushes. Other cacti that look like the **beavertail** but have longer spines are called **prickly-pear** cacti.

ORGAN PIPE CACTUS
Color: Green with whitish flowers in spring and early summer.
Size: 10–26 feet (3–7.9 m) tall.
Notes: This cactus has a lot of stems that come up from the base without a trunk like the **saguaro** or **cardón**. Its flowers open at night and are visited by bats.

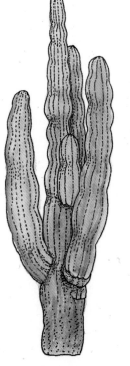

BARREL CACTUS
Color: Green with reddish or yellowish large spines and yellow flowers in the spring.
Size: 3–10 feet (1–3 m) tall when fully grown and may be 1 foot (30 cm) in diameter.
Notes: Sometimes these large cacti are easy to spot on rocky slopes and canyon walls, even if you're riding in a car. They look reddish green from a distance.

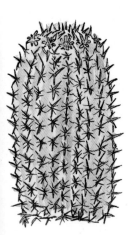

CARDÓN
Color: Light green branches, grayish green trunk with whitish flowers in the spring.
Size: Up to about 50 feet (15.2 m) tall.
Notes: The largest cactus in North America, it is native to Mexico. Its flowers are open during the day. Look for it on bajadas, level plains and rocky hillsides.

SAGUARO
Color: Green with creamy white flowers in the spring.
Size: Up to 50 feet (15.2 m) tall.
Notes: This is a very large and easy-to-spot cactus and its flower is the state flower of Arizona. Saguaros grow very slowly and don't even get branches until they're about 50 years old. When they are young, it is common to find them growing under the branches of a shrub or tree. This "nurse plant" protects the saguaro until it is large enough to survive on its own.

CHOLLA
Color: Green stems with yellowish or whitish spines.
Size: There are several kinds of **cholla**. They grow from about 3 feet (1 m) to 12 feet (3.6 m) tall, or more.
Notes: The stems of chollas sometimes break off and stick to clothes, that's why some are called "jumping chollas." The spines are hard to get out (and they can hurt), so be careful around them. One of the chollas is called "Teddy-bear" because that's what it can look like with the dead brown spines still on the older parts of the plant.

Shrubs

MORMON TEA

Color: Medium green, bluish green, or yellowish, olive-green.
Size: About 3–5 feet. (1–1.5 m) tall.
Notes: This is a "scraggly" bush, made up of jointed green stems and teeny, tiny leaves and flowers. It is very common and was used to make a hot drink by Native Americans.

CREOSOTE BUSH

Color: Dark green. During the spring, it gets lots of small yellow flowers, which turn into white, fuzzy fruits in late spring.
Size: A big bush, 3–12 feet (1–3.6 m) tall.
Notes: This common shrub is found all over the hot deserts of North America. Look on and around it for insects, animal holes and animal tracks.

BRITTLEBUSH

Color: A gray-green bush with yellow, daisy-like flowers.
Size: 3–5 feet (1–1.5 m) tall.
Notes: Commonly seen along highways, desert washes and bajadas.

YUCCA

Color: Dark gray-green or olive-green leaves and creamy white to yellowish flowers.
Size: Many kinds and sizes ranging from about 3 feet (1 m) like the **banana yucca** to **Joshua trees**, which are over 15 feet (4.5 m) tall.
Notes: Look for lots of narrow, long leaves coming out from a base or trunk. The leaves end in spines, so be careful … getting stuck with a yucca leaf really hurts! (The yucca flower is the state flower of New Mexico.)

AGAVE

Color: Commonly yellowish green or grayish green leaves, with yellow, white or greenish flowers.
Size: The cluster of leaves at the base of some of the smaller agaves only grow about 1 foot (30 cm) high. Others can get to be about 4 feet (1.2 m) high.
Notes: The leaves are stiff and thicker than those of the yuccas and can be tipped with sharp spines. These can hurt a lot if you get stuck, just like with the yuccas. This was an important plant for Native Americans, providing them with food, fiber for weaving, and a kind of soap.

OCOTILLO

Color: Gray-to-green stems and green leaves with narrow clusters of red flowers at the tips of the stems (after it has rained).
Size: 8–30 feet (2.4–9.1 m) tall.
Notes: Nothing else looks like an **ocotillo**. They have tall, spiny stems that grow up and out, and are often taller than anything else around them. You will find them on bajadas.

Trees

PALO VERDE

Color: Bluish green or yellowish green trunk and stems, green leaves, and yellow flowers.

Size: 25–30 feet (7.6–9.1 m).

Notes: The green trunk and stems make food for this tree when it's too hot and dry for it to keep its leaves. A large, common tree along washes and low desert slopes, this is the state tree of Arizona.

FAN PALM

Color: Brown trunk and green leaves growing over dead, light brown leaves.

Size: 20–60 feet (6.1–18.3 m).

Notes: These palms will only grow where there is year-round water available. They are often found along earthquake faults, where underground water comes up as springs.

JOSHUA TREE

Color: Brown trunk and branches, dark green leaves, and whitish flowers.

Size: 15–30 feet (4.6–9.1 m).

Notes: Sometimes, there are so many **Joshua trees** growing together, they look like a bizarre, spikey forest. Look for them on level ground and on the lower half of bajadas. And look on and around them for signs of lizards, birds and other animals.

DESERT WILLOW

Color: Light green leaves, dark brown trunk, pinkish flowers.

Size: 25 feet (7.6 m).

Notes: Found most often along washes and riparian areas. Look for something that looks like a huge bush with long, skinny leaves. Provides good cover for birds and animals.

IRONWOOD

Color: Blue-green leaves, gray trunk, and light purple flowers.

Size: 10–30 feet (3–9.1 m).

Notes: This tree gets its name from its very hard wood. It is so hard that cutting it can dull a saw. Look for these trees in washes and on rocky or sandy areas near hillsides.

Animal Tracks

A good way to tell if animals live in an area is to look for animal tracks. This is especially true in the desert where many animals are nocturnal and others only come out very late in the day to escape the heat of the sun. So you could spend an entire day in a desert area and see very few animals. But … if you look around sandy areas in the morning, especially near water, you'll probably find the footprints of things like insects, birds, snakes, lizards, rabbits, **kit foxes**, **coyotes**, and maybe **bighorn sheep** or **pronghorn antelope**. Learning to recognize which tracks belong to which animals can make exploring the desert even more fun.

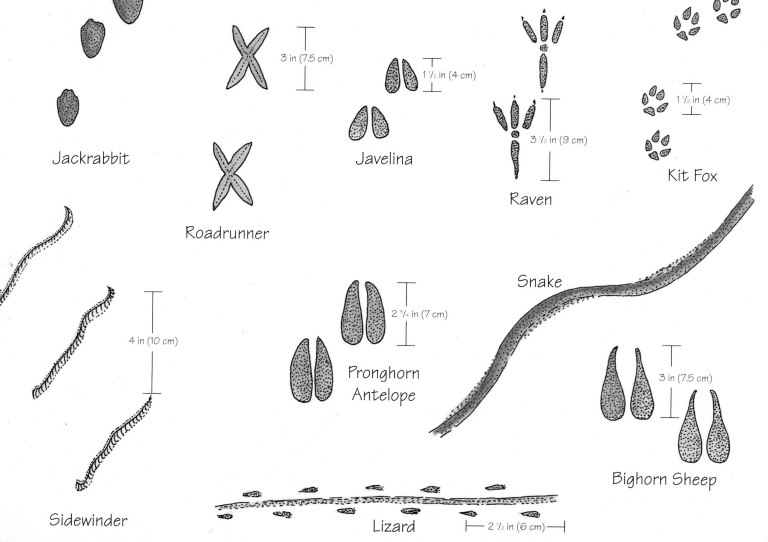

Beetle

Jackrabbit
2 ½ in (6 cm)

Roadrunner
3 in (7.5 cm)

Javelina
1 ½ in (4 cm)

Raven
3 ½ in (9 cm)

Kit Fox
1 ½ in (4 cm)

Sidewinder
4 in (10 cm)

Pronghorn Antelope
2 ¾ in (7 cm)

Snake

Bighorn Sheep
3 in (7.5 cm)

Lizard
2 ½ in (6 cm)

Glossary

Adapt: Changing the way you live or do things to survive better in a different or changing environment.

Bajada: A sloped area of rocks, gravel and sand that have washed out of the adjacent mountains.

Burrow: An underground animal home dug out of sand and/or dirt.

Carnivore: An animal that eats other animals.

Diurnal: Refers to an animal active during the daytime.

Dune: A hill of sand or other tiny particles that shifts around in strong winds and has very little plant or animal life.

Elevation: Refers to the number of feet or meters a place is above or below the level of the ocean.

Environment: The large area (sky, rocks, dirt, etc.) that makes up a plant or animal's home.

Evaporation: Refers to the process by which liquid water changes into a gas and escapes into the air.

Habitat: The environment that is home to an animal or plant.

Herbivore: An animal that eats plant material.

Nocturnal: Refers to an animal that is active during the night.

Omnivore: An animal that eats both plants and animals.

Parasite: An animal or plant that sometimes lives on the body of another plant or animal.

Playa: A dry, low-lying area (often with salty soil) that can become a temporary shallow lake after it rains.

Predator: An animal that hunts other animals.

Prey: An animal that is hunted by other animals.

Riparian: A habitat area that has some type of water available to plants and animals year-round.

Wash: A sandy and/or rocky channel that water flows through during desert rains. It is dry most of the time.

Pronunciation of Some Desert Words

Bajada (ba-HA-da)
Javelina (ha-ve-LEE-na)
Ocotillo (o-ko-TEE-o)
Chihuahuan (chi-WHA-whan)
Lechuguilla (lech-oo-GE-a)
Playa (PLY-a)
Cholla (CHO-ya)
Mesquite (mess-KEET)
Saguaro (suh-WAH-row)
Gila (HEE-la)
Mojave (mo-HA-vee)

Resources

CHIHUAHUAN DESERT
Big Bend National Park
Texas 79834
(915) 477-2251

White Sands National Monument
19955 Hwy 70
Alamogordo, New Mexico 88310
(505) 479-6124

SONORAN DESERT
Arizona-Sonora Desert Museum
2021 North Kinney Road
Tucson, Arizona 85743
(520) 883-2702 (recorded info)
(520) 883-1380

Organ Pipe Cactus National Monument
Route 1, Box 100
Ajo, Arizona 85321
(602) 387-6849

Desert Botanical Garden
1201 North Galvin Parkway
Phoenix, Arizona, 85008
(602) 941-1217 (recorded info)
(602) 941-1225

GREAT BASIN DESERT
Great Basin National Park
Baker, Nevada 89311
(702) 234-7331
(702) 234-7270 (Great Basin Natural History Association)

COLORADO DESERT
Living Desert Wildlife and Botanical Park
47-900 Portola Avenue
Palm Desert, California 92260
(619) 346-5694

Palm Springs Desert Museum
101 Museum Drive
Palm Springs, California 92262
(619) 325-7186

Anza-Borrego Desert State Park
200 Palm Canyon Drive
Borrego Springs, California 92004
(619) 767-4684

MOJAVE DESERT
Joshua Tree National Park
74485 National Park Drive
Twentynine Palms, California 92277
(619) 367-7511

California Desert Information Center
831 Barstow Road
Barstow, California 92311
(619) 255-8760

DEATH VALLEY
Death Valley National Park
P.O. Box 579
Death Valley, California 92328
(619) 786-2331

List of Common and Scientific Names

If you're visiting the Sonoran or Chihuahuan Deserts in the United States, you might see an animal that looks like a hairy pig called a "Javelina." And if you tried to look up this animal in a book, you might also find it called a "Collared Peccary." Common names for plants and animals may be different depending upon who you hear them from and where you're looking. But everywhere, all over the world, the *same* scientific name is used for a particular plant or animal.

Scientific names have two parts, both underlined. The first part is called the **genus** and is capitalized, and the second part is called the species and is not capitalized. So the scientific name for the Javelina (or Collared Peccary) is written: *Dicotyles tajacu.* (When you see "**spp.**" used after the **genus** name, it means that there's more than one kind of that plant or animal).

The following list includes all the plants and animals illustrated in this book.

Agave (*Agave* spp.)
Ant (many different genera and species)
Antelope Squirrel (*Ammospermophilus* spp.)
Antillean Blue Butterfly (*Hemiargus ceraunus*)
Antlion or Doodlebug (Brachynemurus spp.)
Arizona Blister Beetle (*Lytta magister*)
Arrow Weed (*Pluchea sericea*)
Banana Yucca (*Yucca baccata*)
Bark Scorpion or Sculptured Centruroides (*Centruroides sculpturatus*)
Barrel Cactus (*Ferocactus cylindraceus*)
Bat (many different genera and species)
Beavertail Cactus (*Opuntia basilaris*)
Big Sagebrush (*Artemisia tridentata*)
Bighorn Sheep (*Ovis canadensis*)
Black-tailed Jackrabbit (*Lepus californicus*)
Bobcat (*Felis rufus*)
Boojum or Cirio (*Fouquieria columnaris*)
Brittlebush (*Encelia farinosa*)
Burrowing Owl (*Speotyto cunicularia*)
Cactus Wren (*Campylorhynchus brunneicapillus*)
California or Mexican Poppy (*Eschscholzia californica*)
Camel Cricket (*Macrobaenetes* spp.)
Cardón (*Pachycereus pringlei*)
Catclaw Acacia (*Acacia greggii*)
Centipede (many different genera)

Chain-fruit Cholla (*Opuntia fulgida*)
Chuckwalla (*Sauromalus obesus*)
Chuparosa (*Justica californica*)
Claret Cup Cactus (*Echinocereus triglochidiatus*)
Coachwhip (*Masticophis flagellum*)
Coati, Coatimundi or Chulu (*Nasua nasua*)
Collared Lizard (*Crotaphytus* spp.)
Costa's Hummingbird (*Calypte costae*)
Cottontail Rabbit (*Sylvilagus audubonii*)
Cottontop Cactus (*Echinocactus polycephalus*)
Cottonwood (*Populus* spp.)
Cougar or Mountain Lion (*Felis concolor*)
Coyote (*Canis latrans*)
Coyote Melon (*Cucurbita palmata*)
Creosote Bush (*Larrea tridentata*)
Desert Agave (*Agave deserti*)
Desert Dandelion (*Malacothrix glabrata*)
Desert Five-spot (*Eremalche rotundifolia*)
Desert Gold (*Linanthus aureus*)
Desert Hairy Scorpion (*Hadrurus arizonensis*)
Desert Holly (*Atriplex hymenelytra*)
Desert Night Lizard (*Xantusia vigilis*)
Desert Spider Beetle (*Cysteodemis armatus*)
Desert Spiny Lizard (*Sceloporus magister*)
Desert-sunflower (*Geraea canescens*)

Desert Tortoise (*Gopherus agassizii*)
Desert Trumpet (*Eriogonum inflatum*)
Desert Willow (*Chilopsis linearis*)
Elephant Tree (*Bursera microphylla*)
Evening Primrose (*Oenothera deltoides*)
Fish-hook Cactus (*Mammillaria tetrancistra*)
Fan Palm (*Washingtonia filifera*)
Gambel's Quail (*Callipepla gambelii*)
Gila Monster (*Heloderma suspectum*)
Gila Woodpecker (*Melanerpes uropygialis*)
Globemallow (*Spaeralcea* spp.)
Golden Eagle (*Aquila chrysaetos*)
Goldfields (*Lasthenia* spp.)
Greater Roadrunner (*Geococcyx californianus*)
Green Sea Turtle (*Chelonia mydas*)
Harris' Hawk (*Parabuteo unicinctus*)
Harvester Ant (*Pogonomyrmex* spp.)
Hedgehog Cactus (*Echinocereus engelmannii*)
Horned Lark (*Eremophila alpestris*)
Horned Lizard (*Phrynosoma* spp.)
Indian Paintbrush (*Castilleja angustifolia*)
Indian Ricegrass (*Achnatherum hymenoides*)
Indigo Bush (*Psorothamnus schottii*)
Ironwood (*Olneya tesota*)
Javelina or Collared Peccary (*Dicotyles tajacu*)
Jerusalem Cricket (*Stenopelmatus fuscus*)
Jimson Weed (*Datura wrightii*)
Joshua Tree (*Yucca brevifolia*)
Juniper (*Juniperus* spp.)
Kangaroo Rat (*Dipodomys* spp.)
Kingsnake (*Lampropeltis* spp.)
Kit Fox (*Vulpes macrotis*)
Ladder-backed Woodpecker (*Picoides scalaris*)
Lechuguilla (*Agave lecheguilla*)
Lesser Nighthawk (*Chordeiles acutipennis*)
Linanthus (*Linanthus* spp.)
Lupine (*Lupinus* spp.)
Marmot (*Marmota fleviventris*)
Mesquite (*Prosopis* spp.)
Mojave-aster (*Xylorhiza tortifolia*)
Mojave Yucca (*Yucca schidigera*)
Monkeyflower (*Mimulus bigelovii*)
Mormon Tea (*Ephedra* spp.)
Mourning Dove (*Zenaida macroura*)
Mule Deer (*Odocoileus hemionus*)
Nevada Buck-moth (*Hemileuca nevadensis*)
Ocotillo (*Fouquieria splendens*)
Organ Pipe Cactus (*Lemaireocereus thurberi*)
Owl's-clover (*Castilleja exserta*)
Painted Lady (*Vanessa cardui*)
Palo Verde (*Cercidium* spp.)
Patchnose Snake (*Salvadora* spp.)

Pencil Cholla (*Opuntia ramosissima*)
Phacelia (*Phacelia* spp.)
Phainopepla (*Phainopepla nitens*)
Pickleweed (*Salicornia rubra*)
Piñon Pine (*Pinus* spp.)
Prince's Plume (*Stanleya pinnata*)
Pocket Mouse (*Perognathus* spp. and *Chaetodipus* spp.)
Ponderosa Pine (*Pinus ponderosa*)
Porcupine (*Erethizon dorsatum*)
Prickly Poppy (*Argemone munita*)
Prickly-pear Cactus (*Opuntia* spp.)
Pronghorn (*Antilocapra americana*)
Pupfish (*Cyprinodon* spp.)
Pyrrhuloxia (*Cardinalis sinuatus*)
Rabbit Brush (*Chrysothamnus* spp.)
Rattlesnake (*Crotalus* spp.)
Raven (*Corvus* spp.)
Red-spotted Toad (*Bufo punctatus*)
Red-tailed Hawk (*Buteo jamaicensis*)
Ringtail Cat (*Bassariscus astutus*)
Rock Nettle (*Eucnide urens*)
Sage Grouse (*Centrocercus urophasianus*)
Saguaro (*Carnegiea gigantea*)
Saltbush (*Atriplex canescens*)
Saltgrass (*Distichlis spicata*)
Sand Food (*Pholisma sonorae*)
Sand Verbena (*Abronia villosa*)
Scaled Quail (*Callipepla squamata*)
Scott's Oriole (*Icterus parisorum*)
Shad-scale (*Atriplex canescens*)
Side-blotched Lizard (*Uta stansburiana*)
Sidewinder (*Crotalus cerastes*)
Silver or Golden Cholla (*Opuntia echinocarpa*)
Skunk (*Mephitis* spp.)
Smoke Tree (*Psorothamnus spinosus*)
Snout Beetle (*Scyphophorus* spp.)
Soaptree Yucca (*Yucca elata*)
Sotol (*Dasylirion wheeleri*)
Spadefoot Toad (*Scaphiopus* spp.)
Stink Beetle (*Eleodes* spp.)
Sun Cups (*Camissonia* spp.)
Tamarisk (*Tamarix* spp.)
Tarantula (*Aphonopelma chalcodes*)
Tarantula Hawk Wasp (*Hemipepsis* spp.)
Teddy-bear Cholla (*Opuntia bigelovii*)
Tree Cholla (*Opuntia imbricata*)
Turkey Vulture (*Cathartes aura*)
Velvet Ant (*Dasymutilla* spp.)
Western Whiptail (*Cnemidophorus tigris*)
White-lined Sphinx Moth (*Hyles lineata*)
Woodrat (*Neotoma lepida*)
Yucca Moth (*Tegeticula* spp.)

Index